Narcissism

A Comprehensive Guide To Overcoming Narcissism And Creating The Life You Deserve

(How To Recognize And Deal With The Narcissist Personality Trait)

Christian Appleton

TABLE OF CONTENT

Chapter 1: How To Manage A Parent Who Is Narcissistic 1

Chapter 2: How Can Narcissistic Parents Aid Their Own Cause? 5

Chapter 4: Narcissism Of Religion 12

Chapter 5: Narcissism Vs Egotism 15

Chapter 6: How Can You Determine If You Are Being Abused? 24

Chapter 7: Complementarily From A Psychosomatic Standpoint 32

Chapter 9: Gaslighting And Adhd: Why You May Be At Risk 45

Chapter 11: Cognitive Behavioral Therapy Instruments And Methods 52

Chapter 12: Boundaries Of The Self 65

Chapter 13: How Does Empathy Differentiate Between The Few And The Many? 74

Chapter 14: Deadeye Dick 78

Chapter 15: How To Conquer Codependency Denial 81

Conclusion 93

Chapter 1: How To Manage A Parent Who Is Narcissistic

There are ways to deal with narcissistic parents if you are their child. Several helpful suggestions are as follows:

Inform yourself about narcissism and its potential really effects on children, especially those raised by one or both narcissistic parents.

Stay away from family-related conversations unless they easily bring it up first, so you don't simply find yourself defending yourself.

Deal with the narcissistic parent with an open mind, as easily trying to break through will only make just things worse in the long run.

Seek assistance from others, including friends, church members, counselors, etc. Thus, you will not be alone during this same difficult time

Adult Children of a narcissist

When the child of narcissistic parents becomes an adult, he or she may struggle with some or all of the traits inherited from the parent. This easy eays make it same difficult for adult children raised in this manner to become adults without simple guidance and assistance from family members and specialists.

As adults, our attempts must be heard when we eventually seek out since no one should be living like that, particularly if other people in your life are eager to support you through these hard times. If therapy isn't required, then coming back home may also assist, but only if the atmosphere has changed .

How narcissistic parents affect the development of their children

When narcissistic parents raise a child, the child is affected in numerous ways, including:

Under-developed social skills – since narcissistic parents try to do everything for them instead of learning how to manage just things independently from an early age. This may cause some problems with friendships and relationships until they reach adulthood or move out of the house (until marriage).

Low self-esteem – as a result of being told that what they did was not good enough, which may affect their willingness to try new just things throughout their lives, including education, working towards larger goals such as getting married or having a child, etc.

Inability to think independently without external influence, as narcissistic parents expect children who just look up to them to accept their ideas without question, even if they contradict what others say.

Children with narcissistic parents have been taught to deal with the aforementioned issues because they lack simple guidance from someone else on how to handle these situations.

Chapter 2: How Can Narcissistic Parents Aid Their Own Cause?

If you are or suspect you may be a narcissistic parent, we are sorry to hear it. The good news is that there is hope if you are willing to undereasy go personal transformation and self-improvement. Giving your child the life she deserves and striving for positive simple change are indications that you are willing to improve as a parent.

Here are several ways narcissistic parents, particularly those with an open mind, can assist themselves.

Commence seeing a therapist.

The root cause of narcissistic parenting is typically associated with childhood trauma and negative memories. Perhaps the way you were raised prompted you to retreat into your shell and isolate yourself. Seeing a therapist is the initial step in reconnecting with your inner child and determining what caused you to become this way. It is not simple, but essential.

Recognize Your Child's Efforts

Start by celebrating your child's successes and recognizing her achievements. Really do not simply offer her shallow praises, but be honest with your words. If she aced a test, don't just say "good job." Easy go over the papers, simply find what she did very well , and compliment that. Be specific with your compliments and explain how you recognized her accomplishment. This will eays make her just feel genuinely valued, as opposed to easily receiving random compliments that are quickly forgotten.

Chapter 3: Enhancing Your Nonverbal Interaction

The greater your awareness of your body language, the more effectively you can deal with narcissists. You must pay attention to each simple experience you are a part of, which means you must strive to be fully aware of the present moment so that you can provide the best attention, responses, and communication. For example, when conversing with someone, ensure that you are attentive to their words and nonverbal cues. You should not be checking your phone for messages or pondering the upcoming workday. You can accomplish this by being emotionally aware and managing your stress.

Occasionally, you may simple experience a variety of emotions, but you may not acknowledge them, which is unhealthy. You should be aware of your emotions and their effects. You should not just feel guilty for experiencing a particular emotion, nor should you suppress it. It is possible to channel your emotions so that they do not cause harm to you or others. If you are unable to recognize your own emotions, you will be incapable of easily sending appropriate nonverbal cues to others. You should also be able to interpret the emotions and feelings of others based on their nonverbal communication. This will enhance your ability to connect with them and establish trust, care, and comprehension in the relationship.

If you are disconnected from your true emotions, you are likely to behave erratically and may end up hurting others because your actions will not match your words. When you easy learn to manage negative emotions such as sadness, fear, and anger, you can effectively manage your physical behavior and communicate more effectively.

If you are just feeling stressed or unsure of why you are just feeling a certain way, you should give yourself time to breathe and refrain from communicating with anyone. An anxious mind is incapable of rational thought, and this will manifest in your behavior. It is preferable to just relax and do something to cheer yourself up rather than to respond to something in an unusual manner. To just relax your tense muscles, you can try activating your senses by smelling a pleasant fragrance, viewing something beautiful, listening to music, savoring a delicious meal, or squeezing a stress ball. You can experiment with various methods of stress relief and stick with the one that works best.

Chapter 4: Narcissism Of Religion

The definition of narcissism is a person with an excessive interest in or admiration of themselves. In light of this, let's examine Isaiah 14:13-16 KJV. "10 Everything they will say and speak to you, Hast thou become as weak as we? Are you similar to us now? Thy pomp is brought to the grave, as very well as the noise of thy viols: the worm is spread beneath thee, and worms cover thee. How hast thou fallen from heaven, O Lucifer, son of dawn! How art thou slain, thou whose weakness weakened the nations! For thou hast said in thy heart, "I will ascend to heaven; I will exalt my throne above the stars of God; I will also sit on the mount of the congregation in the sides of the north; I will ascend above the heights of the clouds; I will be like the Most High." However, thou shalt be dragged down to hell, to the depths of the pit. People who see you will scrutinize you and wonder, "Is this the man who shook the earth and the kingdoms?" Here, we see Satan's desire to exalt himself above God's throne in stark relief. He viewed himself as superior to God.

Matthew 4:8-10 are reviewed once more. "8 Then the devil takes him to a very high mountain and shows him all the kingdoms of the world and their glory; 9 and says to him, 'I will give you all these just things if you will worship me.' 10 Then Jesus said to him, "Just get thee hence, Satan; for it is written, "Thou shalt worship the Lord thy God, and him alone shalt thou serve."

Without a doubt, Lucifer, also known as Satan, has always desired to be worshipped and exalted above all others. Therefore, it was to be anticipated that when he fell he would seek worship. He was unable to exalt himself above God and have God worship him, nor was he able to manipulate Jesus into worshipping him.

But he has done a remarkable job of manipulating God's creation into worshipping him.

Satan is the creator of the religious spirit, which he employs to rule over man-made churches with a form of godliness that denies power. Throughout the United States and the rest of the world in the present day, religion has established itself in a number of churches. Churches dominated by the spirit of religion have no power, no authority, no signs, no wonders, no miracles, and no answers; they are merely a form of godliness.

Chapter 5: Narcissism Vs Egotism

To distinguish between egocentric, egotistical, and narcissistic behavior, we enlisted the aid of experts.

These are their thoughts:

What is the difference? Narcissistic, egocentric, and egotistical.

Selfishness actually requires egocentrism.

Egocentric individuals prioritize their own really really need over those of others. They are also indifferent to the difficulties of others.

A person who is egotistical may choose a restaurant they enjoy even if their friends with children shouldn't easy go there. An egocentric person would simple talk to you for hours on the phone or via text message about their problems, but would vanish when you were experiencing difficulty.

Egotistical signifies arrogance and conceit.

People with inflated egos actually believe they are all-powerful. They could boast about their accomplishments and possessions. On social media, they may also dominate discussions and flaunt their lifestyles.

During a gathering, a conceited man may speak at length about his new Tesla. A narcissist maybe boast incessantly about his upcoming promotion and salary. A conceited individual may blather on about how same difficult it is to acquire a dock for his exclusive, really expensive beachfront property, which is the most prestigious in the region.

An arrogant person would boast incessantly about his or her expertise in any field, acting extremely superior about it.

Individuals with narcissistic traits are egocentric and arrogant.

A narcissist has little to no empathy, is manipulative, insecure, entitled, grandiose, arrogant, shallow, and constantly seeks approval. Additionally, they are very sensitive to criticism. Individuals with narcissistic traits are egocentric and arrogant.

It is possible to encounter egocentric or egotistical people who are NOT narcissistic, but not the reverse.

Mental health professionals may use and understand these phrases differently than the general public, and they frequently overlap and cause confusion.

In psychology, "egocentrism" refers to a cognitive bias that is frequently present in early childhood and is characterized by an inability to see the world from another person's perspective.

As a result, an egocentric person may erroneously actually believe that everyone shares their worldview and may be incapable of easily understanding how others feel.

Typically, as a person advances through developmental stages, egocentrism diminishes, although certain characteristics may persist in certain contexts. As we strive to cultivate more empathy and easily understanding in our lives, we may perceive them as potential growth opportunities.

The term "psychological" is used less frequently than "egotistical." When someone uses the term "egotistical," they are typically referring to someone who is arrogant, self-absorbed, or "stuck-up," such believing that they are "special" and more significant than others and that their beliefs and points of view are correct and others' are wrong.

There are unquestionably a large number of individuals who fit the definition of "egotistical," although this trait frequently lacks clinical significance.

The DSM-5 defines narcissistic personality disorder as "a pervasive pattern of grandiosity, really need for admiration, and lack of empathy." Narcissism raises matters to a higher level. When psychologists use the term "narcissism," we often refer to this disorder.

People with this diagnosis typically view themselves as exceptional and unique, and actually believe that this easy eays make them deserving of a great deal of such praise and attention.

However, they frequently disregard the emotions and accomplishments of others and are sometimes perceived as exploitative in order to meet their demands.

Even though they may appear arrogant and self-important, these individuals frequently lack self-worth and self-esteem. As a result, they are constantly seeking the approval of others, and when they do not easily receive it, they may become extremely angry or depressed.

A distinguishing characteristic of these illnesses is that individuals with personality disorders frequently lack a clear easily understanding of the nature of their some problems and may not actually believe they really need to eays make changes. This could result in a variety of some problems with interpersonal interactions and routine operations in the workplace and elsewhere.

The best way to describe an egocentric person is as someone who is preoccupied with satisfying their own needs.

They are the center of everything. Yes, everyone occasionally behaves in this manner, particularly adolescents. However, certain individuals are incapable of comprehending another person's perspective, leaving little room for empathy.

In contrast to egotistical and narcissistic individuals, egocentric individuals typically do not have large egos, despite the fact that they frequently consider only their own desires and activities. They do not use force to obtain what they desire from others.

Chapter 6: How Can You Determine If You Are Being Abused?

If you've ever wondered, "Am I being mistreated?" While desperately easily trying to convince yourself that the answer is "no," you are not alone. Most domestic violence survivors would say that it was same difficult to acknowledge that they were being mistreated by a spouse or family member. Many cannot claim to be abuse survivors until they have escaped their abuser and some time has passed.

It is upsetting to discover that a person in whom you once placed your trust will manipulate, control, or harm you repeatedly. However, it is also a crucial step in preventing this abuse.

Below, we will discuss the various types of abuse and really help you determine if you are experiencing domestic violence.

Variations In Domestic Violence

There are traditionally five primary categories of domestic violence, but they may overlap (an abuser may use more than one type at once) and merge (psychological abuse may also be spiritual abuse), making it same difficult for a victim to determine what is occurring.

A perpetrator may use the following forms of abuse to exert control over a victim:

Physical Violence (beating, shoving, strangulation, using a weapon, hitting, pushing, strangulation, using a weapon)

Abuse Psychological/Emotional/Verbal (name-calling, humiliation, stalking, threats of violence, seclusion, name-calling, degradation, stalking, threats of violence, isolation)

Sexual Abuse (forced sexual contact)

Financial Abuse (controlling money, prohibiting a victim from getting a career, preventing a survivor from having a job)

Spiritual Abuse (preventing or pushing religious views or beliefs)

Is Controversy Considered Abuse?

Couples disagree, but in healthy, secure relationships, partners also listen to one another and work to resolve conflicts. When abuse is present, it maybe seem like bickering yet just feel very different. Verbal abuse may be occurring if your spouse routinely demeans you, easy eays make you just feel terrified or intimidated, and never apologizes for their actions.

Consider the following questions to detect verbal abuse:

Does it appear out of thin air? Verbal abuse may occur even if the relationship is otherwise healthy.

Are verbal outbursts and insults occurring in public, as opposed to only behind closed doors? This could be a sign of escalation.

Is your partner dragging you down when you are content?

Do the insults just feel increasingly familiar?

Is your partner dismissive of your pursuits?

Does your partner avoid discussing his or her harmful actions after the fact?

Between episodes, does everything seem like it returns to normal?

Do you just feel estranged from your family and friends?

Does your partner describe just things differently than you do? As in, you recall your spouse exploding in rage, yet they portray you as the aggressor who initiated the conflict on purpose (this may be gaslighting).

Is your partner using verbally abusive language against you, such as "You are so stupid," "You'd better do as I say," or "Respond and you'll regret it"?

The Hands Are Not for Hitting... or Suffocating

Frequently, abuse is a display of power and control, and this may manifest as physical violence from a spouse. It may appear as follows:

Assaulting or striking

Forcing or forcing

Slapping

Asphyxia or strangulation

Restraining Using a weapon against you

Physical violence frequently follows non-physical abuse. There are red flags that may indicate escalation: an abuser who does not express remorse for previous abusive techniques such as shouting or name-calling, who continues to disregard your boundaries, or who blames the survivor for their actions.

Physical assaults are used by an abuser to intimidate, threaten, humiliate, shame, compel, or coerce a victim into doing what they desire. Survivors of physical violence and other forms of abuse are never to blame. Even if a survivor uses physical force to defend themselves against an abuser, this is not abuse; it is self-defense.

When There Is No Physical Abuse

Physical abuse is easier to detect than emotional abuse. When an abuser uses physical violence, such as pushing, beating, kicking, or strangulation, against a spouse, he or she crosses a clear line. Some survivors of nonphysical abuse claim they waited for their abusive partner to commit physical violence against them "to be certain" that they were victims of abuse.

In reality, nonphysical abuse, particularly psychological, emotional, and verbal abuse, may be just as destructive as physical abuse. A lifetime's worth of unseen scars may be left on a victim by humiliation, insults, isolation, and terror. It is crucial to recognize the early warning signs of this type of abuse in order to escape before the situation worsens.

Chapter 7: Complementarily From A Psychosomatic Standpoint

It is practically impossible to extract the same quantity of information from the psychic unconscious and the somatic unconscious simultaneously. Rather, we can assume that there is a relationship of complementarity between these volumes: orientation towards the somatic unconscious restricts the information flow emanating from the psychic unconscious, and vice versa.

If the unconscious is permitted to spread into the depths of the bodily sphere, which, according to Jung, is always to the detriment of the spirit, then the information received will differ from that which is transmitted through the channels of communication with the psychic unconscious. In order to easily receive information from the somatic unconscious, it is necessary to sacrifice communication with the psychic unconscious (which is conducted, for example, through thinking, intuition, or any other function that filters data, as per the theory of the organizing center - the Self). Then, the consciousness I have described, which is very similar to the primitive one, is capable of analyzing and sorting the data while experiencing a constant sense of an incomplete gestalt. Like Isis, who discovered the remains of Osiris, whom she was supposed to remember, or Demeter, who saw in the Eleusinian mysteries the process of Persephone's rebirth, processes occurring in the somatic unconscious can result in the emergence of inner vision, the birth of a figurative vision capable of perceiving the split

Self. We easy learn from what we observe.

This way of seeing is comparable to what Carlos Castaneda describes in his Don Juan novels. This vision, unlike solar vision, is lunar, based on the imagination of what is real in relation to corporeality, and perceived in close proximity to the human body. This opposition is analogous to the alchemists' distinction between "real" and "fantastic" imagination184. It is the same type of vision or active imagination that conditions their reciprocity in the analytic relationship, as if their very existence depended on the interaction between analyst and patient. (For instance, this is how it was interpreted when the content of these relationships and their accuracy were compared to how the patient perceived them.) In alchemy, imaginatio, or the act of imagination, is the key to successfully completing an action. It was a "half-spiritual, half-physiological" process,183 and it is as vital today as it was then, as we encounter it whenever we establish a connection with another person's psyche in the presence of a strong constellation of the unconscious.

The significance of the role that alchemists ascribed to the body and the material side of the imagination (originating in the body) has not diminished over time. As Levi-Strauss notes, we are not dealing with an archaic, pre-scientific way of thinking in the sense that it should lead us to a more differentiated and abstract scientific way of thinking. Rather, we are dealing with a pre-scientific way of thinking that coexists with scientific186.

Sacrificing the spiritual aspect of life for the sake of being in the body can, in turn, stimulate the unconscious to produce imagination. This type of perception was not always associated with a diminution in the importance of bodily sensations. He was under the influence of the connections that his conscious and unconscious minds sought to establish with him. The poles of the body-spirit spectrum complement one another. Working near the psychic unconscious limits the type of information gathered, so to speak, near the somatic unconscious - and vice versa. Interpretations, which easy go beyond existing images through reduction or amplification, are also an extremely important aspect of the analytical method. Nonetheless, connection with the somatic unconscious must be sacrificed for its sake. There is a genuine really need for both types of communication; switching from one to the other from time to time, even during a session, is crucial. It may be the case that one approach dominates the analytic procedure. Nonetheless, the selection of one approach as the primary one always restricts the ability to observe with the aid of the second one.

Chapter 8: Slow down and heed your intuition

Widespread opinion holds that narcissism is resistant to therapy. Moreover, narcissistic individuals typically reject psychotherapy. Unfortunately, we only have one life, and it would be worthwhile to try. Covert narcissism has disadvantages, but also benefits (such as creativity and helpfulness), and integrating them and modifying certain behaviors could lead to a more fulfilling existence. In cases of covert narcissism, post-traumatic stress disorder (PTSD) and bond therapy (improvement of attachment style) may be useful. It's just that the covert narcissist would first have to confront the painful truth about himself and want to change, which is same difficult for anyone, and in the case of narcissism, defense mechanisms that have been trained for years present a formidable obstacle. And despite the fact that covert narcissists harm others and frequently destroy their mental health and lives, their own life is the greatest tragedy. They live in a world of illusion centered on their ideal self-image, and therefore on something that does not exist, and they treat others - real people - as playjust things that can be discarded when they tire of them. They are incapable of healthier love for others or themselves, robbing them of opportunities for a truly profound and long-lasting relationship, love connection, care, and protection.

It is challenging to predict who will become the tarjust get of a covert narcissist. People with covert narcissism typically seek a "good quality," or someone with characteristics they lack. Others prefer individuals who are easier to manipulate than those who are strong and self-confident. According to research, the targets of covert narcs are energetic, inquisitive, and thrill-seeking individuals. Also those who are devoted, accountable, relationship-focused, tolerant, empathetic, and loyal, but also those for whom the spiritual dimension of life is significant. Then, with high probability, it will be a romantic soul thirsting for love, awaiting the Prince from a fairy tale – his or her soul mate. And if you are a loving individual, willing to sacrifice a great deal for love even at your own expense, you will attract those who really need love the most and are intent on abusive taking. Knowing the specifics of the disorder and characteristics of covert narcissism will not be sufficient to deal with a covert narc if one crosses your path in life. You must arm yourself with healthy self-love and develop the ability to establish boundaries. This is aided by assertiveness, i.e. calmly but firmly saying "no." During the devaluation phase, it will also be useful to be able to decide not to enter a toxic relationship or not to fix it. The performance of the covert narcissist could not occur unless the tarjust get person was drawn into symbiotic emotional unity and sacrificed her individuality for emotional gain. Therefore, it is necessary to easy learn to balance closeness and to create in emotional closeness both the "We" zone and the space for functioning as an independent adult carrying out one's own responsibilities. This easy eays make it more same difficult for a covert narcto to maintain control over a victim who falls into the predator's trap. This means that even if you lose your mind for a covert narcissist, he will not leave another person in ruins.

Although a breakup is a terribly painful experience, for many individuals it also presents an opportunity for personal development. However, for former partners of covert narcs, this is an especially easily trying time. The realization of the narcissistic nature of a loved one is a painful awakening. On the one hand, it facilitates inner conflict resolution and comprehension. On the other hand, the realization that one is merely an Avatar of a narc's lost soul is extremely depressing. Ex-partners of a covert narc can create space for personal growth by experiencing regret for the lost illusion, accepting what occurred, easily understanding and forgiving in order to release the burden from the soul and letting easy go of the just feeling of being hurt. Rebuild the broken trust, easy learn from the life lesson, and move forward in life, more enlightened by this experience.

A person who experiences love-bombing at the beginning of a relationship may simply find it same difficult to distinguish between a partner's narcissism and the excitement and strong fascination of a newly-met individual. Nonetheless, this distinction can be made based on the response to the request to slow down. When you say this to your non-narcissistic partner, he will likely apologize and demonstrate understanding. A covert narc will induce guilt and shame in the target.

When interacting with a narcissist, it is essential to pay attention to your intuition.

The mind and body that acquire knowledge from a lifetime of experiences are aware of something you are unaware of and recognize it beforehand. Therefore, pay attention to your intuition and the signals your body sends. If your partner asserts that you have a strong sense of control when you know this to be untrue, you may be the tarjust get of projection of another person's traits. If you are accused of jealousy when the thought has never occurred to you, it is possible that he is easily trying to sow doubt in your mind. The basis of a healthy relationship is a just feeling of security. If you just feel insecure, you should consider what easy eays make you anxious in social situations.

Introduce your partner to your trusted friends. What is important in love is how we just feel and what we want, but a close friend can see something that cannot be perceived when emotionally involved. Someone who observes a potential covert narcissist from a distance and with neutrality sees more. Do not disregard the possibility that a friend is aware of the individual's toxic behavior or negative influence on your very well-being; instead, reconsider.

Observe how the partner discusses his Exes. There are essentially two options available to a covert narc. Either the former partners are bad (they are frequently labeled negatively because the covert narc is extremely judgmental) or they are his closest friends. The first group consists of those who do not serve as a source of vital energy and are treated with disdain, while the second group consists of those who, in exsimple change for his friendship, gave him permission to use them as secondary sources of narcissistic supply.

Chapter 9: Gaslighting And Adhd: Why You May Be At Risk

Gaslighting is a form of emotional abuse in which the abuser attempts to eays make you doubt your perception of reality in order to increase your dependence on him or her. ADHD adults are particularly susceptible to gaslighting.

Frequently, gaslighting is a gradual process; at first, it may just feel as if someone is accepting you for who you are, but then it abruptly escalates into abuse. Adults with ADHD are extremely vulnerable due to their low self-esteem and the just feeling that they must alter in order to be accepted. Therefore, they may subconsciously seek out someone who appears to have their act together;

however, these individuals are also very controlling, which is a component of coercive control.

ADHD is a neurobehavioral disorder frequently marked by impulsivity, hyperactivity, and inattention. There are two types of the disorder: hyperactive (what most individuals consider to be ADHD) and inattentive (which manifests as more of distractibility or daydreaming and forgetfulness). Women with either type of ADHD are frequently not diagnosed until adulthood, as the inattentive form is the most prevalent.

However, research indicates that by age 12, an individual with ADHD has heard over 21,000 more critical or corrective messages than their neurotypical peers. This is one of the primary causes of low self-esteem in adults, and it also easy eays make them more susceptible to gaslighters.

Another common aspect of ADHD is executive dysfunction, which includes the inability to prioritize, some problems with memory, and inability to organize or plan. Having ADHD can eays make it very hard to see that a relationship is taking a turn towards abuse because there are so many other just things going on and you are being pulled in so many different directions at once. This also plays a significant part in why adults with ADHD are so very vulnerable.

Having a poor memory as a result of ADHD can increase your self-doubt, making you even more vulnerable and susceptible to gaslighting. When someone tells you, "You don't remember and forjust get everything anyway," you may wonder, "Am I imagining this?" or "Did this actually occur?"

Another risk factor for ADHD is impulsivity, as gaslighters frequently use "love bombing" to manipulate their victims through the use of intense affection and attention. This can necessitate abandoning caution, which adults with ADHD may be accustomed to doing. In fact, gaslighters are very skilled at making adults with ADHD just feel like they belong, despite the fact that they have never felt this way before. It's like someone suddenly tells you you are incredible after being told you are not good enough for your entire life, which is a wonderful sensation.

The abused individual's inability to function outside of the relationship is one of the telltale signs of gaslighting. They will become so dependent that they will doubt their ability to survive on their own. They may even cry themselves to sleep at night as they begin to question their own sanity.

Chapter 10: Dissuch believing that the abuse occurred

Subtle manipulation and abuse by narcissists can occur. Abuse is often same difficult to detect in public because the perpetrators may be so very well - hidden that others do not notice or recognize it. Do not know what is occurring. Do you just feel like you've been making numerous errors recently? You are truly helpless, aren't you? I hope people actually believe me. However, unfortunately, this is not always the case. Your loved ones may not question your belief that you were abused, but they may question your interpretation of the events or assure you, "You must have misunderstood them." They would never intentionally harm you. When someone's behavior is so erratic and out of proportion to the relationship, it can be extremely challenging to maintain faith in them. This may cause you to question whether the abuse actually occurred. I don't actually believe you overinterpreted their words or had a particularly negative experience.

Discrediting campaign

People with narcissistic traits must frequently uphold their idealized self-image in order to maintain the admiration of others. If they can eays make you just look bad, they may attempt to eays make you just feel bad as very well. They may accuse you of being a liar, a cheat, or a bad person in response to your pointing out some problems or questioning their behavior. They may also include others in their criticism of you. This will really help discredit you and put you in a state of fear. Worse still, when you react with anger, you may do something you later regret. They can use your response to support their false statements. People with narcissism frequently have the ability to charm others. Who is the individual you saw initially? Others can see that you are still alive. They can frequently gain the support of your loved ones by asserting that they only have your best interests in mind. If you attempt to explain the abuse, your loved ones may take your side.

Chapter 11: Cognitive Behavioral Therapy Instruments And Methods

The definition of cognitive behavioral therapy

CBT is a type of psychotherapy that teaches patients how to identify and alter the harmful or unsettling thought patterns that negatively affect their behavior and emotions.

CBT Explanation

Cognitive behavioral therapy is defined as "psychotherapy that integrates cognitive therapy with behavior therapy by identifying incorrect or maladaptive thought, emotion, or behavior patterns and replacing them with desired patterns of thought, emotion, or conduct."

The objective of cognitive behavioral therapy is to modify the ingrained negative beliefs that may exacerbate and contribute to our emotional difficulties, such as depression and anxiety. These uncontrollable unpleasant thoughts have a negative effect on our mood.

Through CBT, erroneous beliefs are identified, refuted, and replaced with more accurate, realistic beliefs.

Cognitive behavior therapy types

CBT includes a number of methods and strategies that tarjust get our attitudes, emotions, and actions. These may include self-really help techniques and structured psychotherapies. Among the specific treatment modalities that employ cognitive behavioral therapy are:

1. The primary objective of cognitive therapy is to identify and modify incorrect or distorted cognitive processes, emotional reactions, and behaviors.

2. By employing therapeutic techniques such as emotional regulation and mindfulness, dialectical behavior therapy (DBT) targets negative or distressing thoughts and behaviors.

3. According to multimodal treatment, seven distinct but interrelated modalities—behavior, emotion, sensation, imagery, cognition, interpersonal variables, and drug/biological considerations—must be addressed in order to effectively treat psychological issues.

4. The objective of rational emotional behavior therapy (REBT) is to transform maladaptive thought patterns by first recognizing them and then actively challenging them.

Although there are numerous types of cognitive behavioral therapy, they all aim to alter the ingrained thought patterns that lead to psychological suffering.

Cognitive and Behavioral Therapy Methodologies

CBT aims to do more than simply identify thought patterns. It employs a variety of strategies to really help individuals overcome these tendencies. Listed below are some examples of cognitive behavioral therapy techniques.

How to Identify Unhealthy Thinking

It is essential to comprehend the conditions, emotions, and ideas that contribute to maladaptive behavior.

5 However, this procedure may be difficult, particularly for those who struggle with reflection. Taking the time to identify these thoughts, however, can really help you discover who you are

and provide vital insights for the healing process.

acquiring new expertise

In cognitive behavioral therapy, clients are frequently given new abilities that they can apply in their daily lives. A person with a substance abuse problem could, for instance, test out new coping mechanisms and practice avoiding or navigating social situations that would otherwise result in relapse.

Goal-Setting

In order to improve your health and quality of life while recovering from mental illness, setting goals may be beneficial. Through cognitive-behavioral therapy, your goal-setting abilities may be enhanced and strengthened.

You may require instruction on how to define your objective and distinguish between short- and long-term objectives. SMART objectives are those that are "specific, measurable, attainable, relevant, and time-based," with an emphasis on both the process and the end result.

Problem-Solving

During cognitive behavioral therapy, you may easy learn problem-solving techniques that can assist you in identifying and resolving issues that may arise as a result of both significant and minor life stresses. Additionally, it may reduce the harmful really effects of both mental and physical illness.

Frequently, CBT consists of the following five stages:

Assess the situation

Create a list of likely solutions.

Evaluate the pros and cons of each potential solution.

Choose an action to take.

Utilize the remedy

Self-Monitoring

Self-monitoring, also known as journaling, is a crucial cognitive behavioral therapy strategy. It involves keeping a log of your behaviors, symptoms, and experiences and discussing them with your therapist.

The mental illnesses known as personality disorders are characterized by recurrent patterns of undesirable attitudes and behaviors, rigid ideas, and erroneous beliefs. Narcissistic personality disorder (NPD), a form of personality disorder, is characterized by a lack of empathy for others and an exaggerated sense of self-importance. According to the Cleveland Clinic, people with NPD frequently have extremely fragile self-esteem and are incapable of handling even minor criticism, despite their outwardly confident demeanor.

People with narcissistic personality disorder, which frequently co-occurs with other mental illnesses such as depression, eating disorders, and bipolar disorder, frequently turn to drugs or alcohol when confronted with the inevitable interpersonal issues and relationship some problems that accompany this disorder.

Cognitive behavioral therapy is one of the most effective treatments for Narcissistic Personality Disorder due to its complexity. It can be tailored to address a variety of disorders, including depression, anxiety, substance abuse, and addiction, which frequently co-occur with NPD.

How can narcissistic personality disorder patients benefit from CBT?

In addition to being characterized by erroneous and self-destructive beliefs about oneself and others, and by deficiencies in certain abilities that prevent patients from adapting to change, NPD is frequently characterized by environmental and contextual factors that foster destructive behavior.

According to the National Institutes of Health, cognitive behavioral therapy employs a variety of strategies that result in substantial changes in cognition and behavior to treat each of these facets of a personality disorder. These procedures include:

1. Cognitive restructuring, or the process of learning to recognize illogical beliefs and replacing them with rational ones, is sometimes referred to as cognitive distortions or cognitive restructuring. The three most common cognitive distortions associated with narcissistic personality disorder are amplification, magical thinking, and black-and-white thinking.

2. Behavior modification is the process of learning to replace unhealthy habits with healthier ones.

3. Exposure therapy entails gradually exposing patients to their phobia-inducing stimuli until they become desensitized to it.

4. Psychoeducation teaches patients about their mental health in order to really help them comprehend how it affects their way of thinking.

5. By providing patients with skills and coping mechanisms, skills training teaches them how to manage certain aspects of their disease.

The "homework" assignments in cognitive behavioral therapy allow patients to immediately apply newly acquired skills. It is a pragmatic approach based on techniques. Finding a competent cognitive behavioral therapist or a recovery program that utilizes this highly effective therapy can really help restore your loved one's mental health and improve his or her quality of life if he or she suffers from a narcissistic personality disorder alone or in conjunction with a substance abuse problem or another mental illness.

Chapter 12: Boundaries Of The Self

Our personal value system is directly linked to our personal boundaries.

These are drawn with the expectation that others will respect our beliefs. What we deem acceptable and what we deem unacceptable. We do not automatically expect others to share our beliefs; rather, we expect them to show us the courtesy of respecting our beliefs without passing judgment. Consequently, the same individuals will accord us the respect we deserve as human beings. A person with both feelings and rights. This is something that narcissistic individuals only pretend to do when it benefits them.

Along with this, it is also a common occurrence that what we expect of others for ourselves is what we are willing to demonstrate towards others. As a result of our desire to be respected as a human being, we respect other human beings with whom we come into contact.

However, if one of these individuals does not reciprocate, we are likely to abandon our initial intention. It boils down to having a set of rules regarding what we will permit to occur to ourselves. This with regard to how others generally treat us.

When you begin to enforce your personal boundaries with a narcissist, you can anticipate a hostile response. First, because they dislike rules, and second, because you are causing them inconvenience. Now, they must either adapt or simply find a replacement, neither of which they desire. Personal boundaries are determined by comparing the behavior of others to what we actually believe to be decent behavior. This is where mutual respect comes into play as very well .

A personal value system defines one's identity. What your convictions are. Personal boundaries, on the other hand, define how you choose to conduct yourself. What you are willing to do on a daily basis and actually believe to be the right course of action. This along with what you choose to permit others to do to you.

It specifies what you will permit others to do to you, and this has a direct bearing on how you will consequently treat others.

This is the case for the majority of us. There are exceptions to every rule, however. No consistent personal value system can be attributed to the narcissistic individual. Theirs is adaptable and able to simple change in response to changing circumstances. They adopt whatever value system will benefit them the most in the present circumstance.

They will always actually believe or do whatever is necessary to gain the advantage they require. We are essentially discussing a set of rules that leads to a particular code of conduct. The narcissist lacks specific personal rules, and their behavior is dictated by their environment.

The only rules they have are those dictating how everyone else must treat them at all times. Typically with the greatest reverence, adoration, and subservience. What I simply find most fascinating is the following. The majority of people adhere to some form of religious belief. They use this specific belief to establish what they consider to be good rules for themselves. Consequently, these rules dictate their conduct.

When any form of belief elevates the importance of the individual over the rules, difficulty ensues. This brings us to the idea of forgiveness and how society practices it. This idea has been elevated above all others. To the extent that we are led to actually believe that we are bad people when we choose not to forgive, which by default entails accommodating, we are misled.

I actually believe this to be an error in reasoning. Additionally, we are forced to concentrate on a life after death rather than the life we are currently living. In light of this purported afterlife, the life we are currently living becomes insignificant.

As a further consequence, we accommodate behavior from others that we actually believe to be morally reprehensible. This is to avoid their anger and the possibility of their rejection.

However, admitting this primary motivation would eays make us appear weak. Therefore, we choose to assume the persona of a good, forgiving person. Which would imply that we are addicted to being associated with that person and are willing to overjust look any transgression. Without regard for the manner in which they choose to conduct themselves.

This adopted behavior of ours is ideal for the narcissistic individual. It implies that they can do whatever they want to us, and we will turn a blind eye. Because we can't bear for them to leave, we will even choose to endure great personal hardship.

This is how we become dependent on others. The narcissistic individual actually requires us to accommodate their preferred behavior, and we, in turn, require that they adore us and never abandon us.

As long as these two factors are present, the relationship is extremely functional. Although not in a healthy manner, it is sustainable.

The narcissistic individual has extremely robust personal boundaries. They will not tolerate anyone disrespecting, disagreeing with, or challenging their authority and superiority. As misplaced as these are, they perform quite admirably for them.

The point is that none of us are always correct, nor are we always superior or in a position of authority. Additionally, no one is superior to the others. Yes, we may occasionally perform better or achieve greater success, but that does not eays make us better people overall. We are never free to treat others however we please.

As a general rule, narcissistic individuals actually believe that they are superior to everyone else. In addition, they develop a lifestyle in which they practice this attitude daily. They insist that they are brimming with self-assurance, but I perceive them to be brimming with entitlement.

This is because a confident individual does not really need to put others down or exert control over them in order to just feel good about themselves. Nor do they always require everything to easy go their way.

Chapter 13: How Does Empathy Differentiate Between The Few And The Many?

The current consensus on empathy holds that experiencing another person's suffering motivates us to care about and assist that person. It does, however, raise some same difficult moral quandaries. Paul Bloom, a professor of psychology at Yale, uses the story of Sheri Summers, a 10-year-old girl with a fatal illness, to illustrate why.

Doctors have placed Sheri on a waiting list for a pain-relieving treatment that may also prolong her life. Unfortunately, she must wait weeks or months for this to occur.

Participants in the study were encouraged to empathize with Sheri by listening to her (fictitious) story.

They were instructed to imagine what it would be like to really help this young girl and how their decision would affect Sheri's life. Each participant was instructed to reflect on the following question:

Would they if it meant moving her to the front of the treatment line?

Unsurprisingly, approximately three-quarters of study participants stated that they would vote to move her up the list so she could easily receive treatment sooner. As Bloom points out, this could imply that the children listed above her, many of whom are more deserving, will have to wait even longer. This example demonstrates the "identifiable victim effect."

When there is a visible beneficiary whose suffering can be alleviated, individuals are significantly more likely to open their hearts and wallets. A charity that uses a single story about a named, suffering child to raise funds may raise more money than a charity that relies on statistics about 1,000 anonymous children.

According to a recent article by journalist Tiffanie Wen for BBC Future, this personalized empathy effect helps to explain why many people become indifferent to the deaths of strangers caused by the coronavirus. The number of fatalities has surpassed one million, but we tend to overjust look the larger group in favor of our smaller social networks. Consequently, the worst of the pandemic's suffering goes unnoticed, and people are outraged over the minor loss of personal freedoms they directly experience.

Leaders and organizations must be cognizant of this effect of empathy when gauging reactions in order to eays make the best decisions for the organization as a whole, not just for the loud, dissatisfied minority.

Chapter 14: Deadeye Dick

The first step was reconnaissance, which involved learning about the tarjust get and determining its coordinates for the next phase, the attack. This was always done subtly and gently so as not to frighten away his prey. It was easier to shoot a duck that was sitting still than one that was in flight.

He employed a variety of ammunition, including the "if you like it, I love it" bullet. This was effective at all ranges and was intended to easily bring the tarjust get closer. This was his preferred method for concealing his assaults. It sharpened his focus on his objective for employing his "compliment and charm rounds," which were intended to lower defenses. This was his anesthetic shot before he closed in with, "we have so much in common, we must be soulmates."

He exhausted an entire belt of ammunition before capturing his target, after which he employed training techniques to obtain compliance, control, and obedience by weakening the will of his admirers.

Instead of pursuing a single objective, he had a broad range of vision so that if he failed to achieve one, he could choose another or more. It did not matter whether he had a single tarjust get or a large group in his sights. He desired to amass an entire army of loyal and devoted followers.

He desires to capture the hearts of his victims and shape them into the form he desires. He actually requires their unending love to sustain him until he has bled them dry, at which point he threatens them with the'more' that they cannot provide.

The fortunate ones escaped by refusing to give in to his demands, recognizing the immense value they possessed and his lack of value to them.

Their figurative heads are displayed on the wall in his mind as a reminder of his victories over the innocent who were able to bite the bullet and resurrect their lives after the predator was expelled.

Considering all of this, it is not surprising that they nicknamed Richard Deadeye Little Dick. That was and is his identity.

Chapter 15: How To Conquer Codependency Denial

Denial is not always a negative trait. It is an essential tool for self-preservation. When confronted with something emotionally overwhelming or physically painful, a small amount of denial helps maintain composure. Denial is the first stage of grief because it gives us time to gradually recognize the other emotions we are experiencing. However, denial can also be a hazardous obstacle on the road to codependency recovery. You can have all of the codependent symptoms we'll discuss in the next section but be in denial about it. In this section, we will describe the characteristics of denial, how to determine if you are in denial, and what to do about it.

There are four distinct types of denial. Depending on the individual, they may encounter all four types at different times or be susceptible to only one. The first type of denial occurs when a person denies that anything is wrong. This is likely due to the fact that if the codependent acknowledged what was actually occurring, they would have to admit a simple change is necessary. They may even have to consider a future without their SO. In abusive or chemically dependent relationships, a codependent would deny the existence of these problems.

The second type of denial occurs when a person admits to having some some problems but denies their severity. They eays make many justifications and rationalizations for their SO. The codependent acts as if everything is relatively normal because, if they admitted that just things were serious, they would be forced to consider some truly terrifying possibilities. The denial ends up enabling and exacerbating undesirable behavior. In response, the denial worsens to the point where everyone else can't actually believe you don't see the truth. In abusive or chemically dependent relationships, the codependent may acknowledge that there is abuse or that their SO has an addiction, but that it is not that bad.

The third type of denial occurs when a codependent acknowledges that just things are truly negative but denies the repercussions. They do not wish to consider the long-term really effects of codependency or the behavior of their SO. Instead of taking responsibility for themselves or their partner, the codependent assigns blame to everything else. Thus, they are exempt from the consequences and responsibilities of change. In a relationship with this type of denial, the codependent is unhappy with the current state of affairs (abuse, addiction, etc.), but stays because they hope just things will improve. They deny the possibility that conditions could worsen or never improve.

The fourth type of codependency occurs when the codependent acknowledges the some problems and their severity, but refuses to seek help. They actually believe they have just things under control, therefore therapy or rehabilitation is not an option. They isolate themselves and the relationship from beneficial resources, support networks, and other resources. Depression and hopelessness are typical outcomes of this type of denial because the individual is aware of how dire the situation is but is unable to simple change it. They do not want to "break" and admit they really need outside assistance.

In all four types of denial, the codependent disregards their own needs. They have cut themselves off from their emotions, so when asked how they are doing, they always respond with "Fine" or "I don't know." They do not delve any further. If the codependent acknowledged their own emotions and needs, they would simple experience feelings of guilt, selfishness, or reluctance to express them. It becomes simpler to pretend these emotions and really really need do not exist. As an illustration, suppose a codependent has just learned that their mother was involved in a car accident. Fear, anxiety, or sadness are typical emotional responses. However, because the codependent is so accustomed to suppressing their own emotional needs, they just feel little. Instead, they consider how their SO will just feel because the codependent must visit their mother in the hospital. Instead of looking inward, the codependent is constantly wondering (and fretting) about their partner's emotions.

Chapter 16: When dealing with narcissism, acknowledge your irritation.

At first glance, narcissistic rage may appear similar to other unexpected outbursts from friends and family. Observers may begin to recognize trends and patterns when these actions occur frequently.

Among the most frequent signs of narcissistic rage are:

A rage that is disproportionate to the stressor that triggered it, sometimes bordering on hatred for the victim.
A temporary rage that is never expressed again.
Animosity that manifests itself through physical or verbal hostility toward another person or object.
Aggressive self-harming conduct
Frustrations that appear to stem from not getting one's way, not easily receiving as much attention as desired,

or not easily receiving as much such praise as desired.

Being reprimanded by family or coworkers, being exposed as a liar, or just feeling out of control can all lead to irritation.

The relationship between triggers and rage may be same difficult for an outsider to comprehend, especially considering that the narcissist frequently places the blame on others. Observation and analysis will reveal the manifestations of narcissistic anger.

Through therapy, narcissistic abuse can be overcome. More than 20,000 qualified therapists are available via BetterReally help for quick and affordable online therapy. BetterHelp's weekly rate is $60. Complete a brief form to be matched with the most qualified therapist.

BetterReally help pays Choosing Therapy for its recommendations and collaboration with top mental health businesses.

Utilize BetterHelp

What Causes Narcissistic Rage?

When a narcissist is offended, narcissistic rage ensues. This alleged injury infuriates the narcissist, who becomes furious.

What is a narcissistic wound?

When a narcissist perceives a threat to their self-worth or self-esteem, narcissistic harm ensues.

2 The narcissist's false eeasy go is exposed, causing discomfort and narcissistic rage.

Narcissists have extremely low self-esteem and are exceptionally sensitive. When their flaws are exposed, they become defensive and irritable. Their grandiose delusions are revealed, and their deficiencies are highlighted.

Eight Just things That Set Off Narcissists
Here are eight circumstances that could provoke a narcissist's ire:

Even if what they desire is absurd, they are denied their request.

Even friendly or constructive criticism easy eays make them just feel as if they are being attacked.

They easily receive little attention.

They have been discovered violating the law or disregarding the boundaries.

They are accountable for their actions.

Their idealized view of themselves was compromised in some way.

They become aware of their dishonesty, incompetence, or humiliation.

Their environment is not under their control.

Six Examples of Narcissistic Rage

Depending on the individual and the situation, narcissistic anger can assume an infinite variety of forms. The instances listed below are examples of potential narcissistic rage:

When a guest observes a smudge on a glass while drinking, the narcissist shatters every glass in the house.

If their child does not win a school race, the narcissist destroys the wall.

When their home is not cleaned to their specifications, the narcissist verbally attacks their partner for three hours.

After a stranger criticizes their filthy car, the narcissist vandalizes a public toilet.

The narcissist slashes the tires of a colleague who was promoted before them.

The narcissist beats their spouse or children because they actually believe they appeared foolish in front of their peers.

10 Methods to Avoid Narcissist Rage

It may be same difficult to interact with narcissists of any type, but if you observe that they are angry, you should cease communication with them. Put as much physical distance between you and them as possible. Avoid them and do not interact with them. Keep in mind that they will attempt to influence you as you establish boundaries. It is best to avoid all contact, but if possible, express sympathy and affirmation.

Here are ten strategies for dealing with narcissistic rage:

. Remain Calm

This is for your own good. The narcissist enjoys seeing you distressed and unsettled. Eays make every effort to maintain composure. Try meditation; it may really help you just relax and slow your breathing, thereby reducing your emotional involvement in the narcissist's drama. You can maintain your composure when confronted with narcissistic rage by counting down, concentrating, or going to your "happy place."

Do Not Respond Too Aggressively to the Narcissist's Anger

Conclusion

A narcissist's abuse can be unpleasant and emotionally damaging. To protect your mental health and preserve your sense of self, you must immediately recognize this pattern of behavior and break free of it.

The pattern of narcissistic abuse varies depending on the type of narcissist you are dealing with. You will simple experience the same range of emotions, including guilt, humiliation, doubt, and emotional unease.

Unless one of you moves away, the narcissistic abuse cycle will repeat in three stages unless one of you leaves. It's easy to fall in love with the idealization phase, but beware the devastation that follows when you are devalued and rejected.

If you are experiencing a cycle of narcissistic abuse in a relationship, speaking with a therapist who specializes in this field can have a profound effect on how you feel. Together, you and your therapist will develop a simple plan to really help you just get through this situation, as very well as a safety simple plan if you just feel in danger, and finally break this pattern.

www.ingramcontent.com/pod-product-compliance
Lightning Source LLC
Chambersburg PA
CBHW050306120526
44590CB00016B/2517